Let Freedom Ring

The Women Suffrage Movement, 1848–1920

by Kristin Thoennes Keller

Consultant:
Frances Barbieri
Education Director
Seneca Falls Historical Society
Seneca Falls, New York

Bridgestone Books
an imprint of Capstone Press
Mankato, Minnesota

Bridgestone Books are published by Capstone Press
151 Good Counsel Drive, P.O. Box 669, Mankato, Minnesota 56002
http://www.capstone-press.com

Library of Congress Cataloging-in-Publication Data
Thoennes Keller, Kristin.
    The women suffrage movement, 1848–1920/by Kristin Thoennes Keller.
    p. cm.—(Let freedom ring)
    Summary: Follows the efforts of American women who fought for
women's right to vote and the passage of the nineteenth amendment to the
Constitution.
    Includes bibliographical references and index.
    ISBN 0-7368-1562-7 (hardcover)
1. Women—Suffrage—United States—History—Juvenile literature. [1.
Women—Suffrage. 2. Women's rights—History.] I. Title. II. Series.
JK1898 .T46 2003
324.6'23'0973—dc21   2002010827

Editorial Credits
Angela Kaelberer, editor; Karen Risch, product planning editor; Kia Adams,
    series designer; Juliette Peters, book designer; Angi Gahler, illustrator;
    Kelly Garvin, photo researcher

Photo Credits
Corbis, 20, 29; Bettmann, 9, 15, 38
Hulton Archive by Getty Images, 12
Library of Congress, cover (main), 17, 25, 27, 34, 41, 42
North Wind Picture Archives, 31, 37
Sophia Smith Collection, cover (inset), 43
Stock Montage, Inc., 5, 7, 11, 19, 23
U.S. Postal Service, 14

1   2   3   4   5   6   08   07   06   05   04   03

Table of Contents

Chapter One

The Beginning of the Movement

In June 1840, Elizabeth Cady Stanton met Lucretia Mott at the World Anti-Slavery Convention in London, England. Both American women looked forward to sharing ideas about ways to end slavery. But they and the other women present were not allowed to speak. They had to sit behind a curtain and listen to the men.

The event was important for Stanton and Mott. Neither woman understood why they had fewer rights than men did. Their friendship began the movement for suffrage, or the right to vote, for American women.

Elizabeth Cady Stanton helped start the women's suffrage movement in the United States.

Early American History

In the late 1700s, only white men who owned property could vote in the American colonies of Great Britain. But even these men could not vote for members of Parliament, who made laws for Great Britain and its colonies. Colonists were angry about paying high taxes without having any vote in their government. Colonists began protests against the British government. These protests resulted in the Revolutionary War (1775–1783).

On July 4, 1776, colonial leaders signed the Declaration of Independence. This document declared independence from Britain and stated that "all men are created equal." These words did not apply to American Indians or African American slaves. Nor did they apply to women.

Women had few rights in the late 1700s. A married woman was thought of as her husband's property. Husbands owned women's belongings, land, and money. In some states, women could not even spend money without a husband or a father's permission.

Women did not control their own or their children's lives. Fathers could send children to live with or work for another family. If a married couple divorced, the woman lost all rights to her children. If a man died without a will, his wife usually would receive none of his money or property. Even if a man left a will, his wife would not always get the full amount. The government or the oldest son could receive a share as well.

In 1776, U.S. leaders signed the Declaration of Independence. This document gave equal rights to many American men, but did not mention equal rights for women.

Women Question the New Government

While men fought the Revolutionary War, women began doing what had been thought of as men's work. Women hunted, trapped, farmed, and ran businesses. After the colonies won independence, women began to ask why they did not have the same rights as men did. Women knew they had worked hard to help win the war and form the new country.

Under the new government, each state had different rules about voting rights. For example, Pennsylvania voters did not need to own property. Instead, men who paid taxes were allowed to vote and run for office. In 1783, New Jersey gave some voting rights to women who owned property. But state lawmakers reversed this law in 1807.

Women's Education

In the 1700s, education for girls was limited. Most girls learned to read and write at home. Boys could attend public school and study more subjects.

By the early 1800s, some high schools for girls opened, but these schools rarely taught math and science. In 1821, Emma Hart Willard founded the Troy Female Seminary in Troy, New York. Willard's school was the first to teach math and science to girls. In 1837, Mary Lyon founded Mount Holyoke College in South Hadley, Massachusetts. It was the first women's college in the United States.

As more colleges admitted women, women began careers. Many women became teachers. In 1849, Elizabeth Blackwell, pictured below, became the first woman to graduate from 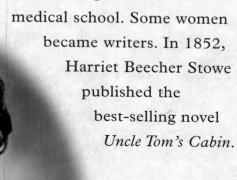 medical school. Some women became writers. In 1852, Harriet Beecher Stowe published the best-selling novel *Uncle Tom's Cabin*.

Chapter Two

Seneca Falls

By the early 1800s, the United States had outlawed the capture and sale of slaves from Africa. Still, owning and selling slaves in the United States was allowed. Many people wanted to end, or abolish, slavery. Many women joined the abolitionist movement.

Lucretia Mott was a Quaker minister who spoke in public against slavery. This activity was dangerous for Mott and other women. Some people became angry with women for speaking in public. These people sometimes threw rocks or eggs at the women or burned the buildings where they spoke.

Women wanted a larger role in the abolitionist movement. Women wrote magazine articles and letters to newspapers about the problems of women and slaves.

Lucretia Mott spent much of her life working to end slavery. In her late 40s, she began working for the suffrage movement.

Sojourner Truth

In May 1851, supporters of women's rights gathered in Akron, Ohio. Several well-known women spoke at the convention, but the most memorable speech was delivered by a woman who could neither read nor write.

Sojourner Truth was born into slavery in the 1790s. She lived through many hardships before becoming free in 1828. In the 1840s, she began making powerful speeches against slavery. When she arrived at the Akron convention, some people did not want her to speak. They worried that Truth would not properly represent the suffrage movement. Frances Gage, who organized the event, allowed Truth to speak.

Truth spoke about the hardships of her life. She said no one had ever given her the special treatment that white women were believed to receive. She asked several times, "Ain't I a woman?" As she spoke, her audience cheered and clapped loudly.

Truth never lived to see equality for women and African Americans. She died in 1883, but people remember her words. Today, her famous speech still is read, quoted, and printed in books and newspapers.

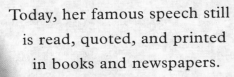

They gathered with other women and men who supported women's rights and abolition of slavery.

First Women's Rights Convention

In 1848, Mott and Elizabeth Cady Stanton decided to hold a convention in Seneca Falls, New York, to talk about women's rights. Mott and Stanton helped write a list of women's demands called the Declaration of Sentiments. The list was based on the Declaration of Independence. It included the right to an education and a career. It said that women should be allowed to own property and share legal custody of their children. Stanton also added the right to vote. She knew women would not be able to control their lives without this right.

More than 300 people, including about 40 men, attended the Seneca Falls convention on July 19 and 20, 1848. Frederick Douglass, a famous African American abolitionist, spoke in support of women's rights at the meeting. The organizers also presented the Declaration of Sentiments. Sixty-eight women and 32 men signed it. One signer, 19-year-old Charlotte Woodward, was the only woman present who lived long enough to vote in a national election. That election did not come until 72 years later.

News of the convention made many people angry. But the convention encouraged women all over the United States to organize their own meetings about women's rights.

In October 1850, more than 1,000 people attended the first National Women's Rights Convention in Worcester, Massachusetts. Lucy Stone, a gifted public speaker, was among them. Stanton and Stone worked well together, but the movement still needed organization.

In 1968, the U.S. Postal Service issued a postage stamp that honored Lucy Stone.

In 1848, Elizabeth Cady Stanton spoke at the first women's rights convention in Seneca Falls, New York.

Chapter Three

Suffrage and the Civil War

In 1851, newspaper editor Amelia Bloomer introduced Stanton to Susan B. Anthony in Seneca Falls. Up to that time, Anthony had devoted most of her time to the abolitionist movement. After meeting Stanton, Anthony spent the rest of her life working for women's rights.

The women's suffrage movement now had the leadership it needed. Stanton wrote speeches, letters, petitions, and articles in support of women's rights. With seven children, she did much of her work at home. Anthony was a good speaker and organizer. Stone and her husband, Henry Blackwell, gave speeches supporting women's suffrage throughout the country. Mott provided support and wisdom to the movement.

In 1851, Elizabeth Cady Stanton, at left, and Susan B. Anthony, at right, began working together for women's suffrage. The photo above shows them later in life.

The Movement Makes Progress

The early suffrage leaders first worked on property rights for married women. Anthony asked 60 women to collect signatures supporting the Married Woman's Property Act. This law would give married women the right to keep their own earnings, write a will, and share custody of their children. In six weeks, the women received 6,000 signatures by going door to door. Anthony asked Stanton to present the women's demands to the government of New York.

In February 1854, Stanton spoke at a women's rights convention in Albany, New York. Anthony printed her speech and sent a copy to each New York legislator. These lawmakers made fun of Stanton in a report.

In spite of this response, the women continued their work. In 1860, Stanton spoke in person to the New York legislature. The next day, the lawmakers passed the Married Woman's Property Act. Other states soon passed similar laws.

Dress Reform for Women

During the 1800s, women's clothing was uncomfortable and made moving difficult. Women wore floor-length dresses with many layers of petticoats underneath.

Early in the 1850s, newspaper editor Amelia Bloomer (pictured at left) began wearing a loose-fitting tunic that ended 4 inches (10 centimeters) below the knee. Underneath the tunic were loose-fitting, ankle-length pants. Many suffragists began wearing these pants, which came to be called "bloomers." But the public refused to accept this change.

Stanton and Anthony thought the clothing took attention away from their suffrage efforts. Suffragists stopped wearing bloomers, but the pants became fashionable again in the 1880s.

The End of Slavery

During the Civil War (1861–1865), suffragists supported the U.S. government and worked to end slavery. Their actions helped convince the states to approve the 13th Amendment to the U.S. Constitution in 1865. This amendment ended slavery in the United States. In 1866, Anthony and Stanton formed the American Equal Rights Association (AERA). The AERA worked for voting rights for both African Americans and women.

The National Woman Suffrage Association (NWSA) did not support the 15th Amendment to the U.S. Constitution.

In 1868, the states approved the 14th Amendment. It defined citizenship and gave all male citizens the right to vote.

In 1869, Congress approved the 15th Amendment, which made voting rights for African Americans more secure. Like the 14th Amendment, the new amendment did not mention women. For this reason, Stanton and Anthony decided to speak out against the 15th Amendment.

A Split in the Suffrage Movement

Not all supporters of women's suffrage agreed with Anthony and Stanton. Lucy Stone was among those who thought voting rights for African American men would lead to suffrage for women.

By 1869, the AERA had split into two groups. Stone and Henry Blackwell formed the American Woman Suffrage Association (AWSA), which supported the 15th Amendment. Stanton and Anthony formed the National Woman Suffrage Association (NWSA). This group was against the 15th Amendment. The amendment became law in 1870, but the suffrage movement remained split for many years.

Chapter Four

Early Victories

The women's suffrage movement gained its first victory in 1869. The territory of Wyoming gave women the right to vote.

Wyoming's action gave new courage to suffragists. On November 1, 1872, Susan B. Anthony was among a group of women who were allowed to register to vote in Rochester, New York. They voted in the election the next week, even though it was against federal and state law.

Anthony's Arrest and Trial

Two weeks later, Anthony was arrested and charged with illegal voting. The three men who allowed the women to register were also arrested.

Anthony's arrest received much attention. During her trial in June 1873, Judge Ward Hunt did not allow Anthony to speak. Hunt excused the jury and

In 1869, women in Wyoming Territory became the first in the United States to vote in all elections.

Wyoming Keeps the Women

In 1890, Wyoming became a state. Washington lawmakers wanted Wyoming to take away women's right to vote, which the territory had granted in 1869. But Wyoming lawmakers said, "We will remain out of the Union a hundred years rather than to come in without the women."

found Anthony guilty. He ordered Anthony to pay a fine of $100, but she never paid it.

A Struggling Movement

After the trial, Anthony and the NWSA turned most of their attention to changing federal voting laws. The AWSA had a different plan. Lucy Stone thought people would more easily accept changes in state voting laws.

Suffragists soon gained some victories. In 1870, women won the right to vote in the territory of Utah. Washington Territory followed in 1883, Colorado in 1893, and Idaho in 1896. But in 1887, the laws allowing women to vote in Utah and Washington were struck down.

The Temperance Movement

Many women supported the temperance movement. This movement urged people not to drink alcohol. Women began singing and praying inside and outside of bars, which were called saloons. Other women marched as they held signs that warned against the effects of alcohol. By picketing the saloons, women hoped to force them out of business.

Women who supported the temperance movement sometimes entered saloons and tried to convince the men inside not to drink alcohol.

In 1874, the protesters formed the Women's Christian Temperance Union (WCTU). With 25,000 members, it became the largest women's group in the country. Frances Willard was the group's president. Willard knew that women needed voting rights to change alcohol laws.

The WCTU helped spread information about the suffrage movement. But the connection between the WCTU and suffrage soon became a problem. Alcohol supporters tried to get lawmakers to vote against laws giving women more rights. They were afraid women's votes would end the sale of alcohol. Many state suffrage bills failed because of this fear.

The NAWSA

During the late 1800s, Anthony and Stanton continued to push lawmakers for federal change. Lucy Stone and her husband worked on their state-by-state approach. As time passed, the women's differences in opinion became less. In 1890, the NWSA and the AWSA joined. They became the National American Woman Suffrage Association (NAWSA).

Stanton, Anthony, and Stone worked together on the NAWSA's goals. Stanton served as the group's president until 1892. Anthony served as the NAWSA's second president until 1900. She gave her last public speech February 15, 1906, which was her 86th birthday. She died one month later. By that time, Mott, Stone, and Stanton also had died. A new generation of suffragists would have to carry on the fight.

Lucy Stone, shown here early in her life, kept her own name when she married Henry Blackwell in 1855. She was one of the first women to do so. In 1890, she helped form the NAWSA. Stone died in 1893.

Chapter Five

A New Beginning

After its first leaders died, the women's suffrage movement lost some of its power. It gained strength when women factory workers joined the movement in the early 1900s. Women worked long hours in unsafe, dirty factories for low wages. They hoped voting rights would help improve their working conditions.

Strikes and Parades

The factory workers used different methods than earlier suffragists had used. They left their jobs and formed picket lines in front of the factories. These strikes sometimes resulted in arrests of the workers. In 1909, about 20,000 women who worked in New York City clothing factories went on strike. The next year, about 40,000 women took part in a strike in Chicago. Suffragists picketed with the factory workers and collected money to free jailed workers.

In New York City, women workers in clothing factories went on strike for better working conditions. These women also supported suffrage.

In 1910, Stanton's daughter, Harriot Stanton Blatch, organized the first suffrage parade in New York City. Hundreds of women marched up Fifth Avenue. They wore yellow sashes with the words "Votes for Women" on them. The suffragists held a Fifth Avenue parade each year.

State-Level Efforts

In 1900, Carrie Chapman Catt became president of the NAWSA. Catt ran the organization until 1904. In 1909, Catt formed the Woman Suffrage Party. The group's goal was to gain suffrage in each state.

Catt's efforts at the state level had some results. Women in Washington won the right to vote in 1910, followed by a close victory in California in 1911. By 1912, Kansas and Oregon had passed women's suffrage laws. In 1913, Illinois women won the right to vote in presidential elections.

In other states, alcohol supporters and factory owners worked against suffrage. They believed women voters would support higher wages and safer working conditions. Some of these men paid voters to change their votes. They also paid election judges to count votes incorrectly.

Alice Paul's New Ideas

In 1912, Alice Paul became the director of the NAWSA's office in Washington, D.C. Paul organized a suffragist parade. On March 3, 1913, about 8,000 suffragists marched down Pennsylvania Avenue. As the women marched, men shouted insults at them. Some men even spit on the women, tripped them, or threw burning cigars at them.

Paul took advantage of the national attention. She collected signatures and held marches. She

Beginning in 1910, suffragists held a parade on Fifth Avenue in New York City each year. The parade shown in the photo took place in 1911.

wanted the attention to force President Woodrow Wilson to support suffrage.

In 1913, Paul formed the Congressional Union (CU). This group urged lawmakers to support a Constitutional amendment that would give women the right to vote. The amendment was called the Anthony Amendment, in honor of Susan B. Anthony. In March 1914, the Senate voted 34 to 35 against the amendment. Even though the suffragists lost, the close vote gave them hope.

Suffragists and President Wilson

In 1916, the Congressional Union became the National Woman's Party. Party members urged Congress and President Wilson to support suffrage. They sent letters and telegrams to the president and Congress members. They also hung a banner from a balcony during Wilson's 1916 speech to Congress. The banner's message asked for Wilson's help to pass women's suffrage.

In January 1917, Paul arranged for women to picket the White House around the clock. The pickets continued for the next three years.

Women Suffrage in the United States, 1919

WASHINGTON
OREGON
MONTANA
IDAHO
WYOMING
NEVADA
UTAH
CALIFORNIA
ARIZONA
NEW MEXICO
NORTH DAKOTA
SOUTH DAKOTA
NEBRASKA
COLORADO
KANSAS
OKLAHOMA
TEXAS
MINNESOTA
WISCONSIN
IOWA
MICHIGAN
ILLINOIS
INDIANA
MISSOURI
ARKANSAS
LOUISIANA
KENTUCKY
TENNESSEE
MISSISSIPPI
ALABAMA
OHIO
WEST VIRGINIA
VIRGINIA
NORTH CAROLINA
SOUTH CAROLINA
GEORGIA
FLORIDA
VERMONT
MAINE
NEW HAMPSHIRE
MASSACHUSETTS
RHODE ISLAND
CONNECTICUT
NEW JERSEY
DELAWARE
MARYLAND
NEW YORK
PENNSYLVANIA

PACIFIC OCEAN

ATLANTIC OCEAN

LEGEND

Full Voting Rights

Some Voting Rights

No Voting Rights

Wartime Arrests

The United States entered World War I (1914–1918) in April 1917. Many people believed the picketers were being disloyal to the United States. Paul refused to stop picketing.

In June 1917, a mob attacked the picketers. Many people were arrested. More than 200 women faced trial. Paul and many others refused to pay their fines and were sent to jails and workhouses.

Suffragists picketed the White House in Washington, D.C., from 1917 until 1920. They hoped to gain President Woodrow Wilson's support.

The women were forced to live under poor conditions. Women shared their jail cells with rats and mice. The food sometimes had worms in it. Workhouses were even worse. Some guards beat women who caused trouble.

News of the women's treatment horrified many people. Some of these people began supporting the suffrage movement. Women came from great distances to take their turn in the picket lines. People sent money to the National Woman's Party.

In November 1917, President Wilson ordered the women set free. He encouraged senators to pass a suffrage amendment, since women had helped with the war effort. Women had been nurses overseas. They had worked in weapons factories. They had held office jobs so men could fight in the war. Their actions convinced Wilson that women supported their country and deserved a voice in governing it.

Chapter Six

Victory at Last

Carrie Chapman Catt continued to work on the state level with the NAWSA. In 1916, Catt put her "Winning Plan" into place. She wanted suffragists in each state to put pressure on their Congress members.

Catt's plan, combined with Alice Paul's efforts, was successful. By the end of 1917, 16 states allowed women to vote. These states included the state with the largest population, New York. Of the 16 states, six allowed women to vote only in presidential elections.

The 19th Amendment

Paul took full credit when the House of Representatives decided to vote on the Anthony Amendment, now called the 19th Amendment. She thought her pickets, hunger strikes, and jail time had finally worked. Catt thought her state-by-state

Carrie Chapman Catt traveled the country in an effort to convince voters in each state to pass suffrage laws.

efforts were responsible for the success. In truth, all efforts helped get the amendment to the House of Representatives.

On January 10, 1918, the House of Representatives voted 274 to 136 to pass the amendment. The passing vote was exactly the two-thirds majority needed, but the suffragists' work was not finished. They also needed two-thirds of the senators to vote for the amendment. Under pressure from suffragists, President Wilson encouraged the

In August 1920, women celebrated the passage of the 19th Amendment to the U.S. Constitution. This amendment gave women in the entire nation the right to vote.

Senate to pass the vote. In the first vote on October 1, 1918, the amendment lost by two votes.

Pressure on the President

Suffragists accused Wilson of not supporting their cause. In December 1918, Wilson went to France for a peace conference. Suffragists tried a new plan to get his attention. Outside the White House, they burned copies of Wilson's speeches. These women were arrested and jailed.

People protested the women's treatment. They sent messages to Wilson in Europe, demanding that he act. In turn, Wilson sent messages to Senate leaders. In a second vote in February 1919, the amendment lost by one vote.

On June 4, 1919, the Senate voted 66 to 30 to pass the 19th Amendment, but women still could not vote. Three-fourths of all states needed to approve the amendment.

On August 23, 1920, Tennessee became the 36th state to approve the amendment. The 19th Amendment became law on August 26, 1920.

African American Women Left Out of the Vote

The 19th Amendment did not provide suffrage for African American women. Especially in the southern states, government officials found ways to prevent African Americans from voting. Voting officials sometimes gave African Americans difficult tests before allowing them to register. African Americans also had to show proof that they paid taxes or owned property. These rules did not apply to white voters. The 19th Amendment did not truly apply to African American women until the Civil Rights movement of the 1950s and 1960s.

National elections took place in November 1920. For the first time, women in all states were allowed to cast their vote for elected officials of the United States.

After the Amendment

Eighty years after the Seneca Falls convention, many of the demands from that meeting had been met. By the 1920s, women could own and inherit property. They could keep their own earnings. They could share custody of their children. They could attend colleges and have careers.

Elizabeth Cady Stanton wisely insisted on including suffrage in those original demands. She and other pioneers of women's suffrage knew women needed to vote in order to change society for the better. Because of the suffragists' efforts, American women today can vote, run for office, and control their own lives.

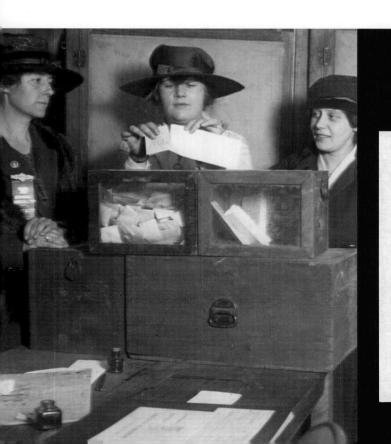

The 19th Amendment allowed women to elect leaders who supported their views. The right to vote allowed women to gain more opportunities in education and the workplace.

TIMELINE

The first women's rights convention is held in Seneca Falls, New York.

14th Amendment gives voting rights to all men.

Elizabeth Cady Stanton and Susan B. Anthony form the American Equal Rights Association.

The states approve the 15th Amendment.

| 1848 | 1860 | 1866 | 1868 | 1869 | 1870 | 1873 |

New York passes the Married Woman's Property Act.

The suffrage movement splits into the NWSA and the AWSA.

Wyoming becomes the first territory to allow women to vote in all elections.

Susan B. Anthony is found guilty of breaking voting laws.

A Constitutional amendment to give women the vote is introduced in Congress, but it does not pass.

Colorado becomes the first state to adopt a state amendment allowing women to vote.

Suffragists begin picketing the White House.

VOTES FOR WOMEN

| 1878 | 1890 | 1893 | 1910 | 1917 | 1920 |

The NWSA and the AWSA join to form the National American Woman Suffrage Association (NAWSA).

The 19th Amendment becomes law after Tennessee becomes the 36th state to approve it.

The first suffrage parade takes place in New York City.

Glossary

abolitionist (ab-uh-LISH-uh-nist)—a person who worked to end slavery before the Civil War

amendment (uh-MEND-muhnt)—a change to a law or a legal document; the 19th Amendment gave women the right to vote.

convention (kuhn-VEN-shuhn)—a meeting of people with the same interests

legislature (LEJ-iss-lay-chur)—a group of people who have the power to make or change laws for a country or state

picket (PIK-it)—to protest by standing outside a place, sometimes trying to prevent people from entering

strike (STRIKE)—a refusal to work until a set of demands is met

suffrage (SUHF-rij)—the right to vote

For Further Reading

Bjornlund, Lydia D. *Women of the Suffrage Movement.* Women in History. San Diego, Calif.: Lucent Books, 2003.

Dumbeck, Kristina. *Leaders of Women's Suffrage.* History Makers. San Diego: Lucent Books, 2001.

Lasky, Kathryn. *A Time for Courage: The Suffragette Diary of Kathleen Bowen.* Dear America. New York: Scholastic, 2002.

Monroe, Judy. *The Nineteenth Amendment: Women's Right to Vote.* The Constitution. Springfield, N.J.: Enslow Publishers, 1998.

Nash, Carol Rust. *The Fight for Women's Right to Vote in American History.* In American History. Springfield, N.J.: Enslow Publishers, 1998.

Price Hossell, Karen. *The Nineteenth Amendment: Women Get the Vote.* Point of Impact. Chicago: Heinemann Library, 2003.

Places of Interest

National Women's Hall of Fame
76 Fall Street
P.O. Box 335
Seneca Falls, NY 13148
This museum honors the contributions of many American women.

Seneca Falls Historical Society
55 Cayuga Street
Seneca Falls, NY 13148
This museum includes photos and documents about the suffrage movement.

Susan B. Anthony House
17 Madison Street
Rochester, NY 14608
Anthony lived in this house from 1866 until her death, and it was the site of her arrest in 1872.

The Women's Museum
3800 Parry Avenue
Dallas, TX 75226
Museum exhibits teach about famous women and important events throughout history.

Women's Rights National Historical Park
136 Fall Street
Seneca Falls, NY 13148
The park includes the home of Elizabeth Cady Stanton and a wall engraved with the Declaration of Sentiments.

Internet Sites

Do you want to learn more about the women's suffrage movement?
Visit the FACT HOUND at *http://www.facthound.com*

FACT HOUND can track down many sites to help you.
All the FACT HOUND sites are hand-selected
by Capstone Press editors. FACT HOUND will fetch the best,
most accurate information to answer your questions.

IT IS EASY! IT IS FUN!
1) Go to *http://www.facthound.com*
2) Type in: 0736815627
3) Click on "FETCH IT" and
   FACT HOUND will put you
   on the trail of several helpful links.

You can also search by subject or book title. So, relax
and let our pal FACT HOUND do the research for you!

Index